# Roisin & the Colourful Garden

**STEPHANIE CULLEN**

**BLUEROSE PUBLISHERS**
India | U.K.

Copyright © Stephanie Cullen 2024

All rights reserved by author. No part of this publication may be reproduced, stored in a retrieval system or transmitted in any form or by any means, electronic, mechanical, photocopying, recording or otherwise, without the prior permission of the author. Although every precaution has been taken to verify the accuracy of the information contained herein, the publisher assume no responsibility for any errors or omissions. No liability is assumed for damages that may result from the use of information contained within.

BlueRose Publishers takes no responsibility for any damages, losses, or liabilities that may arise from the use or misuse of the information, products, or services provided in this publication.

For permissions requests or inquiries regarding this publication, please contact:

BLUEROSE PUBLISHERS
www.BlueRoseONE.com
info@bluerosepublishers.com
+91 8882 898 898
+4407342408967

ISBN: 978-93-5989-783-7

Cover design: Tahira
Typesetting: Tanya Raj Upadhyay

First Edition: January 2024

## Foreword and Acknowledgement

*To all of those that still need to hear that you yourself are just what we need.*

*Thank you so much to all of the friends and family that have helped push me literally every step of the way. I hope this book can be a blessing to you and everyone that needs it.*

# Roisin & the Colourful Garden

*Meet Roisin. A young lass who lives in a beautiful neighbourhood filled with gardens that many from far and wide would come to see. Each neighbour had a beautiful garden of their own, reflecting each one's unique personality.*

*Penelope Purple's garden mesmerised other people walking by with her myriad of vivid purple hues. Even Rickie Red's garden was admired by passers-by even though his temper and bossiness would often scare others off, his garden of radiant reds still pulled in many admirers.*

*Roisin's garden, however, was different. It was grey and gloomy. No leaves of green or vivid purples or radiant reds- in fact, her garden was completely drained of any colour.*

*Roisin watched sadly as she noticed everyone enjoying each other's gardens as well as the many passersby and visitors flocking in to admire and enjoy the plethora of colours and shades their little garden neighbourhood could offer.*

*Silently, Roisin turned back to her garden work after watching her neighbour, George Green, joyfully waving goodbye to his visitors. Suddenly, he happened to glance Roisin's way. She was focused on the shrub she was attending, but appeared sad.*

*The thing that really caught George's attention was the way she was tending the shrub- she was trimming off all of the leaves and flower buds! "Indeed- that is no way to tend to a shrub!" George thought to himself as he walked over to his saddened neighbour.*

"Hey there, neighbour!" George cheerfully greeted Roisin, who responded with a small smile. Curiously, he asked, "Roisin, why are you taking care of this shrub like this?"

"Oh!" Roisin responded, glancing down at the shrub and then back at George. "This is how I was taught," she said matter of factually. "This is how you were taught to take care of a garden?" George asked in bewilderment. "Yes!" Roisin began, "you see…" she paused, thinking about her next words carefully.

"I was told my leaves were too bright and the colour of my roses were too vivid and well... colourful- I was even told that roses were a bad choice for my garden, actually," she explained, nervously.

"Every time I accidentally forgot a leaf or missed a rosebud, others would tear them off and scold me for allowing such things to grow," she finished, and then continued to clip away the new leaves and flowers growing on the shrub.

*George walked away astounded. Why would others scold someone for having a colourful garden? And why teach them the only way to get acceptance was by destroying it?*

*"Who would do such a thing and why?" George thought to himself as he paced back and forth at the foot of his bed. "I need to help her somehow- help her recover her garden," he continued, keeping the rhythm of his pacing all night.*

*Owen Orange's roosters' call rang out in the cool morning sun, causing George to pull away from his thoughts and dash out his front door. He had managed to come up with a plan last night and had already talked to the other neighbours about it. He could not wait to put their plan into action, though he was also nervous how scared Roisin would respond.*

*He reached Roisin's front door before he had more time to think about it and excitedly knocked on her door, calling out, "Roisin! Roisin! Wake up! Quick!" Roisin rubbed her eyes as she shuffled towards her front door, coffee in hand. She opened the door to find a very chipper and excited George nearly bouncing on her welcome mat.*

*"Roisin!" George exclaimed, "I thought that it'd be nice for everyone to get to know you and introduce themselves as well! You know, just a small BBQ tomorrow evening- just to catch up and hang out. I already confirmed everyone else will be there!" he explained enthusiastically, leaving Roisin blinking in confusion at the sudden invitation.*

*That following evening, Roisin walked nervously to the front door of George Green. At first, she had politely declined, but George had promised it was going to be good. That she'd have "fun" and "enjoying it". Two words she had never really understood. And lost in her thoughts, she quietly knocked on her neighbour's bright green door.*

*George Green opened the front door before Roisin had a chance to finish knocking. "PERFECT! You're here!" George practically yelled, ushering Roisin around to the backyard gate, not even giving Roisin the chance to blink.*

*"Surprise!" Shouts came from the backyard as George opened the gate. Luscious green shades of all varieties filled Roisin's vision as a sparkle of awe filled her eyes. The greens were lightly and warmly lit by elegant garden lights and string lights strategically placed.*

*However, the lights, the liveliness of the garden and happy faces of her neighbours surrounding her turned her sparkle of awe to tears of sadness. It was so beautiful and warm - full of life. Things she had wanted but wasn't allowed to have.*

*Her neighbour's smiles also faded to concern and sadness. George reached out, rubbing Roisin's back. "Hey-hey now. We're here to help, Roisin. We know your garden can and will be just as beautiful- if not even more so- than any other in the world," he said encouragingly, the other neighbours nodding in agreement.*

*"H-help me? B-but how?" Roisin stuttered between sobs, "I'm not allowed to have colour. Or life... if I'm caught having a- any colour o-or life-" she started sobbing again. "That's what we're going to help you with, Roisin," Rickie's stern, solid voice rang out as he stepped forward with sure footing.*

"That's right, Roisin," Petunia Purple softly spoke up, coming alongside George to join in comforting Roisin. "Ya' may not be able to get rid of all the negative folks, Roisin, but we want to help ya' form those happy vibes, so their negativity stays with them and doesn't stick to ya', " Yvonne Yellow's sweet country accent chimed in.

"R-really?" Roisin stumbled between heavy sobs. "Y-you guys would really help me like that? You mean I-I can... I can have my own beautiful garden? Really?" Roisin wiped her eyes before clearing up her face. "Thank you. Thank you all, truly, " she shakily said, filled with deep seated gratitude.

"Thank you all so much for everything," Roisin repeated calmly, relief washing over all the neighbours' faces; the air lifting and filling with life again as they all laughed, enjoying each other's company. Roisin silently and softly smiled to herself, hope and eagerness pushing her forward to start her journey of new beginnings restored.

# The Thinking Spot

1. What was your favourite part of the story?

2. Do you think George understood Roisin's way of trimming her shrub? Why do you think so?

3. Do you sometimes feel like Roisin does?

4. When you do feel that way, what do you do?

5. One good way to feel better is to surround yourself with good friends. Do you have any good friends you can trust?

*Next books in the seven-part series of the Life's Little Adventures series:*

*Book 2: Roisin and Rickie Red's Garden Café*

*Book 3: Roisin and the Orange Farm*

*From Roisin and Rickie Red's Garden Café:*

*As she confirmed her mind that was her que to leave, she recalls the BBQ night that was not so long ago now. The threat of going to what was comfortable- her loneliness and pain- beckoned to her. "'I'll be the first to show you the ropes, Roisin!"' Rickie's booming voice had rung out that evening. Everyone had looked at each other nervously, but Roisin remembers her reply clearly.*

*From Roisin and the Orange Farm:*

*She couldn't believe her eyes! There seemed to every kind of orange tree possible- big oranges, small oranges, sweet smelling ones and very bitter tasting ones- they were all here! Not only were the oranges, orange but so were all the farm animals as well! Chickens, cows...*

*Other writings by Stephanie Cullen to look forward to:*

"The Waning Candlestick: A collection of modern poems about life"

# About the Authour:

*Having been adopted twice, Stephanie Cullen's life has been nothing less than an adventure. With the many ups and downs of her life, she wanted to dedicate and write books that could help every child of any age, be it a young toddler or your own inner child, she wanted to share the life lessons that her rollercoaster of a life has been to empower others to overcome any challenge they face. And to prove that there really are those out there that will fight for you and understand you- you just need to find them.*

*So come along on the adventure with Steph and Roisin as they and yourself embark on what it means to love yourself to your core seed- to understand and accept all the aspects of your personality and to endeavor on being the best version of one's self.*

www.ingramcontent.com/pod-product-compliance
Lightning Source LLC
LaVergne TN
LVRC091553080526
838199LV00081BA/728